☑ **W9-BDL-961**

MYTHICAL CREATURES

Written by Natasha Reed
Illustrated by Angela Kincaid

TOP THAT! Kids™

Copyright © 2005 Top That! Publishing plc
Tide Mill Way, Woodbridge, Suffolk, IP12 IAP, UK
Top That! Kids is a trademark of
Top That! Publishing plc

TYPES OF TALES

A legend is a story or collection of tales which is seen to be historically true but which is actually a mixture of fact and fiction. Myths are tales that describe the views of a culture, such as how the world began, or how humans and animals were created.

A legend is different from a myth because it portrays a human hero instead of a god. Folklore consists of folk tales which are passed on through generations by the spoken word. Stories are told to someone else and then they tell another person, and so on.

Mad Monsters

Lots of tales are rooted in fact, but the truth may have been lost over the centuries. Stories of monsters may be animals that humans haven't yet discovered, for example most of undiscovered Earth lies under water so it is safe to assume that there are many species not known to humans. Giant squid were thought to be myths until the 1870s. Any creatures that have been spotted could have been exaggerated, wrongly remembered or made up. Also, some creatures may be ones

Legend Types

Modern legends deal with leading figures in the world of sport, films and popular music. Urban legends are stories which are told, sometimes even in newspapers, as though they were true but their style and ideas indicate that they are folk tales.

we thought were extinct. The Loch Ness Monster closely resembles the plesiosaur and although it seems unbelievable that an animal could remain unseen for millions of years, it has happened.

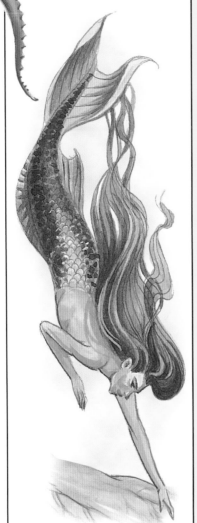

The coelacanth was thought to have been extinct for 70 million years until a South African fishing trawler caught one in 1938.

This book covers the most famous legends, from ancient Greek and Roman mythology to modern myths, and creatures of the sea, woodland, night, air, underworld, folklore and fairy tales, legendary people, as well as both wondrous and evil creatures.

Folklore

This is the often unwritten literature of a people as expressed in folk tales and songs. From the Arthurian Legends of King Arthur and the Round Table, through Bigfoot, Blackbeard, the heroes of Greek legend, and Robin Hood to the Yeti, these are tales that have fascinated us for centuries.

Here's how this book works!

Each section of the book explores a different aspect of our fixation with mythical creatures.

We have included a host of pictures of mythical creatures and important figures in folklore, so that you can become an expert in identifying them and impress all of your friends. However, some of our pictures are missing!

Don't worry though! This is where you need to use the fabulous stickers which are in the middle of the book. When you read about a particular mythical creature match the description to the sticker.

Then, simply put the sticker in the space provided, which will also be labelled with the name of the missing picture.

By the time you reach the end of each section, your head will be crammed full of information. You will also have a great picture to remind you of what you have just learned. In fact, you will be a Sticker Facts mythical creature expert!

SEA CREATURES

Over the years there have been many tales of mysterious sea creatures. These monsters have become today's 'mythical creatures of the deep'.

Sirens

In Greek mythology, the sirens were sea nymphs with the bodies of birds and the heads of women. They were regarded as the daughters of the sea god Phorcys. The sirens had voices of such sweetness that any sailors who heard their songs were lured onto the rocks where the nymphs sang. The Greek hero Odysseus passed by them safely by following the advice of the sorceress Circe

Place your Phorcys sticker here.

and stopping the ears of his companions with wax while tying himself to the mast so that he couldn't go to them. In another legend, the Argonauts escaped the sirens because Orpheus, who was

aboard the *Argo*, sang so sweetly that he drowned out their song. According to later legends, the sirens, angry at the escape of Odysseus and Orpheus, threw themselves into the sea and died.

Sea God

According to Greek mythology, the sea was ruled by the god Poseidon. He was the son of the Titans Cronus and Rhea and the brother of Zeus and Hades. When his brothers divided up the universe after they had removed their father Cronus from power, Poseidon was awarded the sea. Poseidon was the husband of Amphitrite, one of the Nereids, with whom he had a son named Triton. He had numerous other love affairs though, especially with nymphs of springs and fountains, and was the father of several children famous for their wildness and cruelty. Among them were the giant Orion and the cyclops Polyphemus. In Roman mythology Poseidon is called Neptune.

Place your cyclops sticker here.

Terrible Monster

Legend has it that when Poseidon and Apollo, god of the light and music, were cheated of their promised wages after having helped Laomedon, King of Troy, build the walls of that city, Poseidon's revenge against Troy knew no bounds. He sent a terrible sea monster to ravage the land, and during the Trojan War he helped the Greeks.

Shapeshifters

Selkie are a shapeshifting folk that can change from human into seals. It is said that they dwelt in the northern seas around the Orkney Islands.

Kraken

The kraken is described as an enormous whale or turtle-like creature but with tentacles, which could be up to 1.6 km (1 mile) in circumference. It is thought to be real — at least once upon a time. It has not been sighted for more than a century but has in the past been described by naturalists as 'the largest and most surprising of all the animal creations'. On the rare occasions that the kraken makes its way to the surface from the ocean depths, it can easily be mistaken for an island. Occasionally, it would drag down entire ships with its tentacles. It may be dead now, poisoned by marine pollution. Researchers who have studied it claim that it still lives and that it is, in fact sleeping.

Sea Merfolk

In folklore, merfolk are a race of beings with human features above the waist but with the lower body of a fish. They are said to live deep under water, beneath oceans and seas. A mermaid is the young female of the merfolk. She is frequently described as appearing along the surface of the water or sitting on a rock, combing her long hair with one hand while holding a mirror in the other. Mermaids are said to be able to foretell the future, give superhuman powers to human beings, and be able to entice human lovers to follow them beneath the sea.

CREATURES OF THE UNDERWORLD

In ancient Greece it was believed that when mortals died they travelled to the underworld – the mythical realm of Hades and his faithful servants.

Kingdom of the Dead

The Greek underworld was the Kingdom of the Dead. Hades, son of the Titans Cronus and Rhea and the brother of Zeus and Poseidon, was the god of the dead. When Hades' brothers divided up the universe after they had removed their father Cronus from power, Hades was awarded the underworld. He abducted Persephone from above and they ruled the kingdom together. Hades was a god without mercy, and unmoved by prayer or sacrifice, but he was not evil. In fact, he was known also as Pluto, lord of riches, because both crops and precious metals were believed to come from his kingdom below ground. The underworld itself was often called Hades.

Hades Watchdog

The watchdog of the underworld and faithful servant to Hades was Cerberus, a three-headed hound, although sometimes it is claimed it had fifty, with razor teeth, a swarm of snakes growing out of his back and a snake for a tail. Cerberus was said to be the offspring of two monsters, Typhon (a fire-breathing serpent) and Echidna (commonly portrayed as a horrible mixture of beautiful woman and deadly serpent).

Cerberus was so dreadful to look at, anyone who gazed at him turned to stone.

Horrible Harpies

When a person died, they were brought to the underworld by harpies. These were monsters who had the bodies, wings, beaks and sharp talons of

Place your harpies sticker here.

birds and the head of an ugly old crone. They could fly with the speed of the wind and their feathers, which could not be pierced, served as armour. They frequently snatched up mortals and carried them off to Hades, leaving behind them a sickly odour.

Charon the Boatman

Once in the underworld, the first barrier to the soul's journey beyond the grave was the most famous river of the underworld, the Styx. Here, the newly dead waited as shadows of their former selves for Charon the Boatman to ferry them across to the gates of the underworld. He was the aged son of Night and Erebus, who would only take people to the other side on the condition that they were dead and that they had a coin under their tongue as a bribe. Those who had not been buried and whom Charon would not admit to his boat were doomed to wait beside the Styx for another 100 years.

The Labours of Hercules

Another myth involves Hercules. One of his twelve labours was to fetch Cerberus from the underworld. Hades allowed him to take the beast if he caught it with his own hands. Hercules glowered so fiercely at Charon he took him across the Styx. Cerberus was more difficult; he lashed his snakes at Hercules while lunging at his throat. Luckily, the hero was wearing his trusty lion's skin, which could not be penetrated by anything other than a thunderbolt from Zeus. Hercules eventually choked Cerberus into submission and completed the labour. Afterwards, he returned the creature to Hades.

Orpheus and Eurydice

There were several myths about Cerberus and Charon. Orpheus was the son of Apollo, god of light and music, who gave Orpheus the lyre. He became so good that when he played, everyone and everything was moved. After he married the lovely nymph Eurydice, she was stung by a viper and died. Overwhelmed with grief, Orpheus was determined to get to the underworld and try to bring her back, something no mortal had ever done before. With his music, he charmed Charon and Cerberus to enter the land of the dead. The god Hades was so moved by Orpheus' playing that he gave Eurydice back to Orpheus on condition that he did not look back until he reached the land of the living. Orpheus was too eager, however, and glanced back a moment too soon. Eurydice turned back into a ghost again and sank down into Hades' kingdom forever.

NIGHT-TIME CREATURES

Haunting the minds of people after the lights go out, night-time creatures have fuelled our imaginations and frightened the wits out of us for centuries!

Blood Sucker

Throughout history, people have told stories of man-like demons that feed off blood in the night. Vampires are corpses that rise from the grave in the night, often in the form of a

bat, to suck the blood of sleeping humans for nourishment. Most vampire legends were born in the Middle Ages because of fear of the black plague, and ignorance. The most famous legend is the story of Dracula. Various talismans and potions, such as holy water or a crucifix, are supposed to ward

off vampires but, according to tradition, they can be destroyed only by cremation or a stake through the

heart. The modern portrayal of a vampire is a tall, thin man with a white face and fangs, dressed in a black suit and a long black cape.

Russian Bird

The firebird comes from Russian folklore. It is a miraculous bird whose feathers shine silver and gold and whose eyes sparkle like crystals. It is a nocturnal bird and at night it illuminates the land that it flies over. It is said that a feather from its tail can light up a dark room.

The firebird eats golden apples. When it sings, pearls fall from its beak. It is also able to heal the sick and cure the blind by its chants.

Azeman

The azeman originate from South America. They take the form of a human female during the day but at night they transform into a

bat. They feed by draining the blood from their victims. Obsessed with counting, the azeman will stop to count all the seeds scattered on the floor if dropped. It is thought that some of the modern vampire tales come from the azeman.

Black Shuck

During a storm in 1577, a black hell hound appeared at St Mary's church at Bungay in Suffolk, England. Lit by flashes of fire, it ran about the body of the church causing great fear and panic. About seven miles away, at around the same time, it appeared at Blythburgh Church and killed many people. Its claw marks can still be seen on the church's North door!

Dreadful Dog

The barghest comes from northern England and is a monstrous dog with huge teeth and claws. It appeared only at night and it was believed that anyone who saw such a dog clearly would die soon afterwards. In Wales, the dog was called the red-eyed Gwyllgi, the Dog of Darkness. On the Isle of Man it was called Mauthe Doog.

Man Wolf

Werewolves are humans that shape-shift into a wolf or into a half-wolf form, according to ancient superstition. They tend to transform during the full moon and they roam around at night, devouring infants or corpses. The term lycanthropy is a psychological illness where humans believe they are actually wolves.

There are many other voluntary or involuntary transformations; from man to bears, big cats, hyenas and other fierce creatures. Often werewolfism is passed on through tainted blood and can only be ended in death. Shooting them with silver bullets, splashing them with holy water, or forcing them to drink salt water is often said to kill them.

CREATURES OF THE AIR

Swooping down through the ages, mythical creatures of the sky have been central to the beliefs of many different cultures.

Magic Bird

The phoenix was a fabulous legendary bird that lived in Arabia. It was said to be as large as an eagle, with brilliant scarlet and gold plumage and a melodious cry. It was said that only one phoenix existed at any one time and it was very long-lived: up to 500 years. As its end approached, the bird made a nest of aromatic branches and spices, set it on fire and was consumed in the flames. A new, young phoenix then rose from its ashes.

In the mythology of ancient Egypt, the phoenix represented the sun, which dies at night and is reborn in the morning. Early Christian tradition adopted the bird as a symbol of both immortality and resurrection. In Chinese mythology, the phoenix is the symbol of high virtue and grace, power and prosperity.

Sky God

In Greek mythology, Zeus was the god of the sky and ruler of the Olympian gods. Although he did not create either the gods or humans, he was considered to be the father of them. Lord of the sky, the rain god and the cloud gatherer, he wielded the terrible thunderbolt. His breastplate was the protection, his bird the eagle, his tree the oak. Cyclops were giants with just one enormous eye who were thrown into the underworld by their brother Cronus. But Zeus, son of Cronus, released the giants and in gratitude they gave him the gifts of thunder and lightning. With these, Zeus defeated Cronus and the Titans, and became lord of the universe.

Flashing Thunderbird

The thunderbird comes from Native American mythology. It lives among the clouds in the sky and represents the great forces of nature (the Great Spirit). It is a monstrous-sized bird, and so big it can take whales within its talons. When the thunderbird beats its wings they crackle with lightning and rumble like thunder. Arrows of lightning flash from its eyes. Japan also has a thunderbird. It flies about during storms and is connected with the destructive powers of nature, such as thunder and lighting. It also guards the entrance to the sky-heaven.

Arabian Roc

The roc is a legendary creature from Arabian legends. These birds were so big, they could carry off up to three elephants at a time, as well as other large animals and groups of children. The roc is featured in various stories of 'thousand and one nights' and has also featured in the historical texts of Marco Polo on his travels. It lived in the mountains, probably in Persia or India.

Egyptian Ibis

The ibis was a sacred bird from Egypt. It had a white body and black head and tail. It was associated with Thoth

Place your Thoth sticker here.

who was pictured as ibis-headed, as was the moon god Aah on occasions. The bird was sacred to the Egyptian goddess Isis.

Peryton

Believed to be the spirit of travellers who died a long way from home, perytons were originally from Atlantis. They were monstrous stags with wings and light blue, or green, feathers. It is said that they cast the shadow of a man. They would fly in flocks, and attack sailors in the Strait of Gibraltar.

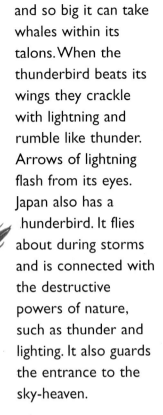

Place your peryton sticker here.

11

FOLKLORE

Past events expressed through songs and tales have been passed down through the ages and become the folklore of today.

The Bogeyman

The bogeymen are creatures from children's folklore which are portrayed as being either really evil or as harmless troublemakers. They can change shape, move objects and cause disruptions. Like ghosts they haunt families, and in some cases they even become friends with the children. They tend to harm those who are liars or someone who

Place your harmless bogeyman sticker here.

commits evil acts. Children are often told that if they are bad, the bogeyman will come to get them.

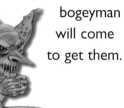

Place your Jack Frost sticker here.

Frosty Looks

Jack Frost is an elfish figure who symbolises crisp, cold wintry weather. He is said to leave patterns in the autumn leaves and the patterns in the frost

left on windows. It is thought that the name Jack Frost comes from Norse mythology as 'Jokul', who was the cause of icicles and 'frosti'.

Will-O'-The Wisps

These are the faint lights seen on marshes and bogs on still nights after sunset. Usually a soft blue light, they are said to lead those who follow them from safe paths into treacherous marshes. The common belief was that they were malevolent spirits, either of the dead, or of non-human intelligence.

Phorcys.

Pegasus.

Kraken.

Robin Hood.

Phoenix.

Prospero.

Dwarf.

Merlin.

Cyclops.

Piper Pan.

Hamadryad.

Mermaid.

Sileni.

Barghest.

Samodivi.

Fairy.

Orc.

Three witches.

Battle of Camlam.

Alien.

Crop circles.

Firebird.

Bat.

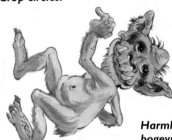

Harmless bogeyman.

Peryton.

Hansel and Gretel.

Charon the Boatman.

Knight.

Cerberus.

Unicorn.

Jack Frost.

Harry Potter.

Dracula.

Holy water
and crucifix.

Thoth.

Harpies.

Thunderbird.

Cornish
pixie.

Hercules.

Griffin
feeding.

Werewolf.

Leprechauns.

Irish Luck

Leprechauns are small sprites that live in farmhouses or in wine cellars. They help humans and do small jobs for them. They ask humans for supplies and furniture, and in return they then give objects that bring luck and fortune. Leprechauns are described as merry little fellows that dress in old-fashioned green clothes and they wear buckled shoes and a red cap.

They are known as fairy cobblers because they make shoes for other elves. They never make a pair of shoes, only one. Popular belief is that a leprechaun possesses a treasure which a human can obtain if they succeed in capturing one, which is very difficult. If you take your eyes off him he will vanish. Leprechauns are mainly found in Irish folklore but they do appear in other countries, too.

Gobble Up

A goblin is an ugly and mischievous sprite, which often has evil intentions. It lives in grottoes or holes in trees, as well as in houses. At night it moves furniture, bangs pots and pans together and snatches the bedclothes off people. Goblins can change shape, often turning into animals. Brownies are good-natured, invisible household goblins. During the night brownies perform household tasks. However, if offered payment for their services, they will disappear and never return.

Cornish Pixie

Pixies are small people who live on the moors of Cornwall, in southern England. According to myth, pixies were originally druids who resisted Christianity, and the more they resisted the smaller they grew. Another myth is that they were a race of people who were not good enough to go to heaven but nor were they bad enough to

go to hell, and were doomed to walk on Earth forever. Pixies are known to steal horses and make night-time trips on them over the moors. They like to trick humans by doing naughty things such as throwing objects around the house. They are hardworking as well, and work in the fields the entire night just to earn some basic food.

Place your Leprechauns sticker here.

WOODLAND CREATURES

The numerous woodland creatures of myth and legend range from the fantastical and magical, to the dark, deadly and dangerous.

Satyrs and Sileni

Satyrs were male creatures who lived in woodlands and forests in Greek mythology. They had horns and tails and sometimes the legs of goats and they resembled the god Pan. The satyrs were the companions of Dionysus, the god of wine, and spent their time pursuing nymphs, and drinking wine, dancing in the woodland and playing the syrinx, flute or bagpipes. In Roman mythology, satyrs were called fauns. Satyrs are sometimes confused with sileni. These are another type of mythological being who look like the satyr, although the sileni sometimes have the ears and tail of a horse. The satyrs however, are represented as eternally young, while the sileni are usually portrayed as older and more mature looking. The most famous of the sileni is Silenus. He

was a wise, elderly, father figure character who, according to legend, tutored the god Dionysus.

Place your sileni sticker here.

Beautiful Bulgarians

The Bulgarian samodivi live in the forest or in the mountain rivers and springs. They fly in long, light, white shirts and ride grey deer, which they whip with snakes. They dance in circles, and their laughter is heard everywhere. The samodivi have beautiful palaces in

Place your samodivi sticker here.

the forest where they grow the samodivi flower, which is called rosen or dittany. They are very beautiful, charming ladies who seek friendship with humans and enchant men. They can bring you suffering, illness or death if you treat them badly but can cure you, too, if you win their mercy.

Treebeard

Treebeard is a character from J.R.R. Tolkien's *The Lord of the Rings*. He is the eldest and most wise of the Ents, an ancient tree-like people. The Ents generally keep to themselves and only look after the trees of the forest. When the wizard Saruman misuses the forest, Treebeard calls the Ents to action and they attack Isengard, Saruman's magical fortress.

Place your hamadryad sticker here.

Woodland Nymphs

Dryads come from Greek mythology and are female spirits or nymphs of nature that preside over the forests. In early legend, each dryad was born with a certain tree species and a particular tree, which she looked after. She lived either in the tree (in which she was called a hamadryad) or near it. Because the dryad died when her tree fell, the gods often punished anyone who destroyed a tree. The name dryad has also been used in a general sense for nymphs who are living in the forest.

Piper Pan

In Greek mythology Pan, the son of Hermes, messenger of the gods, was the god of woods, fields and fertility. He had the horns, hoofs and ears of a goat, and was the god of the shepherds and the goatherds. An especially gifted musician, he accompanied, with his pipe of reeds, the woodland nymphs when they danced. He invented this pipe when the nymph Syrinx, whom he was pursuing, was transformed into a bed of reeds to escape him. Pan took reeds of unequal length and played on them. He was always wooing nymphs by playing on his pipes but was rejected because of his ugliness. He lived in the mountains and caves and many wild places, but his favourite spot was Arcadia where he was born.

Place your Piper Pan sticker here.

FAIRY TALE CREATURES

Many legendary fairy tale creatures, such as dwarves, elves, fairies and trolls originate from German and Scandinavian mythology.

Place your fairy sticker here.

Fairy Fun

Fairies are tiny, supernatural creatures, generally in human form, who live in an imaginary place called Fairyland. Fairies are also said to live in ordinary places such as hills, trees, streams, and the bottom of gardens. In early folk culture, there was a very strong belief in fairies. Fairies are delicate, sensitive, and generally kind towards humans and must always be spoken well of. Sometimes they play pranks. Bad fairies are thought to bewitch children, substituting human babies for ugly, ill-tempered fairy babies (known as changelings).

Dinky Dwarf

Dwarves live under the ground and are very small. They are good fighters with enormous strength. Most live in either Germany or the Swiss mountains. There were seven famous dwarves in the fairy tale *Snow White and the Seven Dwarves*.

Elves

Elves are mythical creatures of German mythology that are frequently pictured in folk tales as small people with mischievous personalities. They were often pictured as living in forests or other natural places, or underground in wells and springs. Elves were imagined to be long-lived or immortal and magical powers were often attributed to them.

Place your dwarf sticker here.

'Orrible Ogre

An ogre is a man-eating giant, typically dim-witted and slow, but very strong. Ogres range in size from 2.7 m to 3.7 m (9 ft to 12 ft). Because of their massive size, ogres are often confused with giants. Ogres are a vicious race that often provoke war against weaker neighbours. The 'giant ogre' has large, tusk-like teeth and is not as smart as the regular ogre.

Terrible Trolls

Trolls are large, underground-dwelling creatures that have a legendary taste for humans. They often did battle with the thunderous Norse god Thor. In certain fairy tales they live under bridges and other dark areas, ready for the unwary traveller to come. In other tales, they live deep inside mountains and hate daylight and noise. Trolls are excellent metalworkers – making fine objects in silver and gold. They enjoy stealing – women and children in particular!

Orcs

In Roman mythology, Orcus, was an alternative name for Pluto, Hades or Dis Pater, god of the land of the dead. In *Orlando Furioso,* by Ludovico Ariosto, the name 'orc' was given to a terrible sea monster. The humanoid, non-marine race of orcs are J.R.R. Tolkien's invention. In *The Lord of the Rings,* Tolkien described orcs as ugly, filthy creatures who are only able to destroy, not create.

Place your orc sticker here.

WONDROUS CREATURES

Exciting, marvellous and dangerous, these wondrous creatures have the advantage of being able to travel through the air.

Deadly Dragon

A dragon is a legendary reptilian monster with wings, huge claws and fiery breath. In ancient folklore, the dragon represented evil and destruction whilst ancient Greeks and Romans believed that dragons had the ability to understand and to convey to humans the secrets of Earth. Used as military symbols because of their fearsome qualities, they are depicted on shields and ships. In China a dragon is traditionally considered to be a sign of good luck and was once the Chinese Empire's national symbol.

Evil Dragon

A relative of the European dragon, the wyvern is a more sinister version. In popular mythology it is seen as an evil and remorseless creature. It is sometimes portrayed with two clawed legs, sometimes four; and is either green or black, with fiery red eyes and foul-smelling breath.

Great Griffin

The griffin is a legendary beast with the head, beak and wings of an eagle, and the body of a lion or tiger. Sometimes it has a tail like a scorpion. It is a fierce and deadly creature that tears its prey apart with its

Place your griffin feeding sticker here.

huge beak while pinning the prey to the ground with one of its talons or paws. Griffins mated for life and if one partner died the other would never re-mate. They were thought to lay their eggs in caves and stood guard over them, to protect them from enemies such as mountain lions.

Trusty Steed

Sleipnir was the swift, eight-legged horse that was able to travel through the sea and air. It served as steed to the great Norse god Odin. This creature was the child of Loki (Norse god trickster) and Svadiffari (the horse that helped build the walls of Asgard), and was given to Odin as a gift. Sleipnir was fast enough to beat any other horse in a race.

Place your Pegasus sticker here.

Winged Horse

In Greek mythology, Pegasus was the winged horse which was the son of Poseidon (god of the sea) and the Gorgon Medusa. Pegasus sprang from Medusa's neck when she was killed by the hero Perseus. Many people tried to catch and tame the horse, without success, and the quest became the obsession of Bellerephon, prince of Corinth. The goddess Athena gave Bellerephon a golden bridle with which he captured Pegasus. The horse became a great help to the hero and aided him on his adventures against the Amazons and the Chimaera. Bellerephon was overcome by his own pride though, and tried to fly to the top of Olympus to join the gods. The wise horse threw him, leaving him to wander alone forever. Pegasus was then entrusted by Zeus to bring him his lightning and thunderbolts.

Pure White

The unicorn is a fabled creature which is pure white in colour. It has the head and legs of a horse and a long, twisted horn in the centre of its forehead. The horn is white at the base, black in the middle and red at the tip. Symbolic of holiness, the unicorn was prominent in many tapestries of the Middle Ages. It was said to have magical powers in healing and the bringing of luck. If a unicorn dips its horn into drink it can tell if the liquid has been poisoned. Legend says that only those most pure in heart and soul, or a young maiden, may be approached by a unicorn.

Place your unicorn sticker here.

WIZARDS AND WITCHES

Wizards and witches are notorious for their ability to wield the forces of magic as they desire, which makes them very powerful indeed.

Prospero

Prospero is the famous wizard in Shakespere's *The Tempest.* He was the Duke of Milan who, with his daughter Miranda, was sent off on a boat, by his brother Antonio, to die. Prospero and Miranda survived and found exile on a small island where he learned sorcery. Because of his powers, some people believe that Prospero represents God.

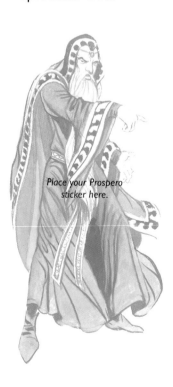

Place your Prospero sticker here.

Harry Potter

Harry Potter is the wizard of today. His exciting stories, written by J.K. Rowling, prove that wizards are alive and well and fascinating children in the same way that they have always done. Harry is the latest in a long line of wizards who use their magic to stop wrong-doing and make the world a safer place in which to live.

Gandalf and Saruman

A character from J.R.R. Tolkien's *The Lord of the Rings,* Saruman came to Middle Earth as the chief of the Istari. For many years, Saruman concealed his secret desires for power and glory. He desired the One Ring, and spent many years preparing armies for war. Gandalf was deemed the most wise of the Istari. He laboured for 2,000 years to put an end to the evil Lord Sauron's reign, and defeated the conspiring Saruman.

The Three Witches – Macbeth

The witches in Macbeth are present in only four scenes, but Macbeth's fascination with them motivates much of the play's action. When they meet with Banquo and Macbeth, they address Macbeth with three titles: thane of Glamis, thane of Cawdor, and king hereafter. Next, they predict that Banquo will father kings, although he will not be king himself. Refusing to answer questions, they vanish.

Place your three witches sticker here.

Sleeping Beauty

Enraged and insulted that the king forgot to invite her to the ceremony celebrating the birth of his daughter Aurora, the evil witch Carabosse announces her curse that the child will one

day prick her finger and die. Luckily, the Lilac Fairy has yet to give her present and declares that although Aurora will prick her finger she will not die. Instead, she will fall into a deep sleep from which she will be awoken after a hundred years by the kiss of a prince.

Hansel and Gretel

Hansel and Gretel is an old fairy tale about a boy and girl who discover a house in a forest which is made of bread, cakes and sugar. The house was inhabited by a wicked witch, who lay in wait for the children. She had only built the house of bread in order to entice the children there so that she could eat them!

Place your Hansel and Gretel sticker here.

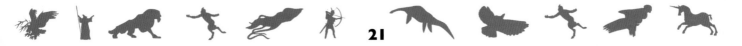

LEGENDARY PEOPLE

The fame of these notorious people have made them a source of exaggerated, and often romantic, tales handed down from earlier times.

King Arthur

Arthur was King of the Britons who fought against the invading Anglo-Saxons. It is unknown whether he was real or fictional.

Place your Battle of Camlan sticker here.

healed of his 'grievous wound'. He possessed a magic sword, Excalibur, which only he could extract from a rock.

According to legend, Arthur was the son of Uther Pendragon, King of Britain. He was a wise and valiant ruler who gathered a great company of knights at his court. He successfully defied the forces of the Roman Empire until he was called home because of the acts of his nephew Mordred, who had rebelled and seized his kingdom. In the final battle of Camlam, England, the king and traitor both fell, pierced by each other's spears. Arthur was mysteriously carried away to the mythical island of Avalon to be

Camelot Castle

With his queen Guinevere, Arthur lived at the legendary Camelot, the most famous castle in the medieval legends of King Arthur. Arthur established a brilliant court at the castle and seated the greatest and most brave

warriors in Europe; the Knights of the Round Table. Camelot was the starting point of the 'Quest for the Holy Grail'.

Place your Merlin sticker here.

Magical Merlin

Merlin started off in legend as a prophet but his role gradually evolved into that of magician, advisor, as well as prophet in King Arthur's kingdom. The legends of Arthur have been re-told so many times over the centuries that the stories have changed almost beyond recognition.

Lancelot

Lancelot was the son of King Ban of Benwick, one of King Arthur's most loyal supporters. When King Ban was defeated in a war and running away, the sight of his home in flames made him faint. His queen Elaine ran to his

side, leaving Lancelot beside a lake. The Lady of the Lake stole the child and raised him in her underwater palace where he was known as Lancelot of the Lake. Other legends say he was stolen by a fairy and raised in Maidenland.

Rich Robber

Robin Hood was the hero in a group of 14th and 15th century English ballads. He was portrayed as an outlaw who lived and poached in the royal forests of Sherwood in Nottinghamshire and Barnsdale in Yorkshire, England. He robbed and killed those the government supported and he championed the cause of the needy and oppressed. His band of comrades included Little John, Will Scarlet and Friar Tuck. It is not known whether Robin

Hood was real or not, but the tales give us a lot of insight into life in medieval times.

MODERN MYTHS

The strange occurrences of today can often be explained by science, but some things cannot. These are destined to be the myths and legends of tomorrow.

Place your crop circles sticker here.

Crop Circles

In 1979, strange circles appeared in some farmers' fields in the UK, created by flattening areas of crop. It was suggested that the patterns were created by aliens in an attempt to communicate with us. More complex patterns emerged years later, but in 1992, two men confessed to creating the first crop circles. A newspaper hired the two men to create another circle, which experts were called in to investigate. They declared it was made by extra terrestrials, proving that people could be fooled.

Nessie

Loch Ness is a long, narrow lake in Scotland. It is reportedly the home of a creature, popularly known as the Loch Ness Monster, but its existence has never been proven. Before there were roads around the loch, there were many sightings by locals and visitors of a strange creature. There were so many tales that, in the 1800s,

records were kept of significant sightings. They were all similar, describing the creature as having a long, strong neck with a small head, a humped back, four short, thick legs, a long tail and huge flippers. It is still not known whether the 'monster' is real or not.

Extra Terrestrials

There have been many tales of aliens in modern times, from long, stick-thin figures with large heads and glowing

Place your alien sticker here.

eyes, to tiny little bugs, to green creatures with many arms and eyes which fly in spaceships. People are fascinated by the idea that there may be life on other planets; intelligent, hostile, friendly, stupid or other. There have been countless stories, books, films and plays about all kinds of extra-terrestrial life, but until we visit more planets, we may never know if we are alone in the universe.

Hairy Being

Also known as the abominable snowman, the yeti is the legendary wild man of the Himalayas. In America, it is called bigfoot and in Canada it is known as sasquatch. There have been many reports of sightings. The creatures are said to be elusive, heavily built, ape-like, hairy, and with facial features resembling a human. They communicate by grunts, cries or whistles. No-one really knows whether the yeti exists, but some people think it is an unknown giant ape, and others believe it is a descendant of prehistoric man. It has also been suggested that the footprints and sightings of yeti were in fact those of snow leopards, foxes, bears or even Tibetan llamas.